POEMS

OF·THE

IRISH
PEOPLE

POEMS
OF · THE
IRISH
PEOPLE

FALL RIVER PRESS

New York

FALL RIVER PRESS

New York

An Imprint of Sterling Publishing Co., Inc.
1166 Avenue of the Americas
New York, NY 10036

Compilation © 2016 by Fall River Press

ISBN: 978-1-4351-6311-9

Manufactured in China

3 5 7 9 10 8 6 4 2

www.sterlingpublishing.com

Cover design by Kelly Thorn
Endpapers: ©Chunhai Cao/iStock

CONTENTS

THE LORE

THE PEOPLE

Introduction

In the introduction to his anthology *A Book of Irish Verse*, published in 1895, William Butler Yeats had this to say about the Irish ballad-makers of the eighteenth century: "The powers that history commemorates are but the coarse effects of influences delicate and vague as the beginning of twilight, and in those days these influences were woven like a web about the hearts of men by farm labourers, peddlers, potato-diggers, hedge schoolmasters, and grinders at the quern, poor wastrels who put the troubles of their native land, or their own happy or unhappy loves, into songs of an extreme beauty." In writing this Yeats was making an observation about the Irish poetic tradition that is borne out by the poems selected for this book: They are inextricably bound up with the lives of the everyday Irish, their love for their country, and their interest in the matters that they hold dear. "Sung" from the heart, these poems and their concerns will resonate with all readers, regardless of their nationality.

Poems of the Irish People is divided into three sections whose boundaries are intentionally imprecise. "The Land" features poems that extol the beauty of Ireland, its breathtaking topography and the towns that are home to its people. As Padraic Colum reminds us, Irish poetry begins with "a dedication of the race to the land": invocations made from the ships of those who settled the land that bound the race to it. One doesn't have to dig too deeply into the vast archives of Irish poetry to find poems dedicated to nearly every town in the country. Some of the most heartfelt poems in this book are written from the viewpoint of expatriates or exiles longing for their native land.

Poems collected in the section entitled "The Lore" pay tribute to the rich legacy of Irish fairy and folk lore. According to the mythic history of Ireland, the Celts who settled Ireland struck a truce with the native Tuatha De Danaan: They would live above ground and the mystical Golden Race below. In this way, the enchantments of Ireland—the fairy folk, the banshee, the leprechaun—are as indigenous to the land as is the Irish race.

In the poems collected as "The People," you will encounter the many persons whom the Irish people comprise: beauties, rogues, heroes, patriots, bereaved mothers, aggrieved lovers—people who are fiercely proud of their heritage and who have borne up stoically under the burdens of oppression and heartbreaking national tragedy. They are the unique character of their own land.

Poems of the Irish People is a celebration of Ireland and the people who call it home. To read these poems, culled from more than twelve centuries of literature, is, as Yeats put it, "to know how strong a wind blows from the ancient legends of Ireland, how vigorous an impulse to create is in her heart."

THE LAND

Ireland

Dora Sigerson Shorter

'Twas the dream of a God,
   And the mould of His hand,
That you shook 'neath His stroke,
That you trembled and broke,
   To this beautiful land.

Here He loosed from His hold
   A brown tumult of wings,
Till the wind on the sea
Bore the strange melody
   Of an island that sings.

He made you all fair,
   You in purple and gold,
You in silver and green,
Till no eye that has seen
   Without love can behold.

I have left you behind
   In the path of the past,
With the white breath of flowers,
With the best of God's hours,
   I have left you at last.

Eire

William Drennan

When Eire first rose from the dark-swelling flood,
God blessed the green island, and saw it was good;
The emerald of Europe, it sparkled and shone,
In the ring of the world, the most precious stone.
In her sun, in her soil, in her station thrice blest,
With her back towards Britain, her face to the west,
Eire stands proudly insular, on her steep shore,
And strikes her high harp 'mid the ocean's deep roar.

But when its soft tones seem to mourn and to weep,
A dark chain of silence is thrown o'er the deep;
At the thought of the past the tears gush from her eyes,
And the pulse of her heart makes her white bosom
    rise.
O! sons of green Eire, lament o'er the time
When religion was war, and our country a crime;
When man in God's image inverted His plan,
And moulded his God in the image of man.

When the interest of state wrought the general woe,
The stranger a friend, and the native a foe;
While the mother rejoiced o'er her children oppressed,
And clasped the invader more close to her breast;
When, with Pale for the body and Pale for the soul,
Church and State joined in compact to conquer the
    whole;

And, as Shannon was stained with Milesian blood,
Eyed each other askance and pronounced it was good.

By the groans that ascend from your forefathers' grave,
For their country thus left to the brute and the slave,
Drive the demon of Bigotry home to his den,
And where Britain made brutes now let Eire make men.
Let my sons like the leaves of the shamrock unite,
A partition of sects from one footstalk of right,
Give each his full share of the earth and the sky,
Nor fatten the slave where the serpent would die.

Alas! for poor Eire, that some are still seen
Who would dye the grass red from their hatred to
    Green;
Yet, O! when you're up and they're down, let them live,
Then yield them that mercy which they would not give.
Arm of Eire, be strong! but be gentle as brave!
And, uplifted to strike, be still ready to save!
Let no feeling of vengeance presume to defile
The cause of, or men of, the Emerald Isle.

The cause it is good, and the men they are true,
And the Green shall outlive both the Orange and Blue!
And the triumphs of Eire her daughters shall share,
With the full swelling chest, and the fair flowing hair.
Their bosom heaves high for the worthy and brave,
But no coward shall rest on that soft-swelling wave;
Men of Eire! awake, and make haste to be blest,
Rise—Arch of the Ocean, and Queen of the West!

The Fair Hills of Eiré, O!

James Clarence Mangan (Translator)

Take a blessing from my heart to the land of my
    birth,
    And the fair Hills of Eiré, O!
And to all that yet survive of Eibhear's tribe on earth,
    On the fair Hills of Eiré, O!
In that land so delightful the wild thrush's lay
Seems to pour a lament forth for Eiré's decay—
Alas! alas! why pine I a thousand miles away
    From the fair Hills of Eiré, O!

The soil is rich and soft—the air is mild and bland,
    Of the fair Hills of Eiré, O!
Her barest rock is greener to me than this rude land—
    O, the fair Hills of Eiré, O!
Her woods are tall and straight, grove rising over
    grove;
Trees flourish in her glens below, and on her heights
    above;
O, in heart and in soul, I shall ever, ever love
    The fair Hills of Eiré, O!

A noble tribe, moreover, are the now hapless Gael,
    On the fair Hills of Eiré, O!
A tribe in battle's hour unused to shrink or fail
    On the fair Hills of Eiré, O!
For this is my lament in bitterness outpoured,

To see them slain or scattered by the Saxon sword:
O, woe of woes, to see a foreign spoiler horde
   On the fair Hills of Eiré, O!

Broad and tall rise the Cruachs in the golden
    morning's glow,
   On the fair Hills of Eiré, O!
O'er her smooth grass for ever sweet cream and
    honey flow
   On the fair Hills of Eiré, O!
Oh, I long, I am pining again to behold
The land that belongs to the brave Gael of old;
Far dearer to my heart than a gift of gems or gold
   Are the fair Hills of Eiré, O!

The dew-drops lie bright 'mid the grass and yellow
    corn
   On the fair Hills of Eiré, O!
The sweet-scented apples blush redly in the morn
   On the fair Hills of Eiré, O!
The water-cress and sorrel fill the vales below;
The streamlets are hush'd, till the evening breezes
    blow,
While the waves of the Suir, noble river! ever flow
   Near the fair Hills of Eiré, O!

A fruitful clime is Eiré's, through valley, meadow, plain,
   And the fair land of Eiré, O!
The very "Bread of Life" is in the yellow grain
   On the fair Hills of Eiré, O!

Far dearer unto me than the tones music yields,
Is the lowing of the kine and the calves in her fields,
And the sunlight that shone long ago on the shields
    Of the Gaels, on the fair Hills of Eiré, O!

The Lake Isle of Innisfree

William Butler Yeats

I will arise and go now, and go to Innisfree,
    And a small cabin build there, of clay and wattles
        made;
Nine bean rows will I have there, a hive for the
        honey bee,
    And live alone in the bee-loud glade.

And I shall have some peace there, for peace comes
        dropping slow,
    Dropping from the veils of the morning to where
        the cricket sings;
There midnight's all a glimmer, and noon a purple glow,
    And evening full of the linnet's wings.

I will arise and go now, for always night and day
    I hear lake water lapping with low sounds by the shore;
While I stand on the roadway, or on the pavements gray,
    I hear it in the deep heart's core.

A Day in Ireland

Michael Cavanagh (Translator)

Four sharp scythes sweeping—in concert keeping
    The rich-robed meadow's broad bosom o'er,
Four strong men mowing, with bright health glowing
    A long green swath spread each man before;
With sinews springing—my keen blade swinging,—
    I strode—the fourth man in that blithe band;
As stalk of corn that summer morn,
    The scythe felt light in my stalwart hand.

Oh, King of Glory! How changed my story,
    Since in youth's noontide—long, long ago,
I mowed that meadow—no cloudy shadow
    Between my brow and the hot sun's glow;
Fair, girls raking the hay—and making
    The fields resound with their laugh and glee,
Their voices ringing—than cuckoo's singing,
    Made music sweeter by far to me.

Bees hovered over the honied clover,
    Then nestward hied upon wings of light;
No use in trying to trace them flying—
    One brief low hum and they're out of sight,
On downy thistle bright insects nestle,
    Or flutter skyward on painted wings,
At times alighting on flowers inviting—
    'Twas pleasant watching the airy things.

From hazel bushes came songs of thrushes
  And blackbirds—sweeter than harper's lay;
While high in ether—with sun-tipped feather—
  The skylark warbled his anthem gay;
With throats distended, sweet linnets blended
  A thousand notes in one glorious chime,
Oh, King Eternal, 'twas life supernal
  In beauteous Erin, that pleasant time.

The Waves of Breffny

Eva Gore-Booth

The grand road from the mountain goes shining
  to the sea,
And there is traffic on it and many a horse and cart;
But the little roads of Cloonagh are dearer far to me
And the little roads of Cloonagh go rambling through
  my heart.

A great storm from the ocean goes shouting o'er
  the hill,
And there is glory in it, and terror on the wind;
But the haunted air of twilight is very strange and
  still,
And the little winds of twilight are dearer to my
  mind.

The great waves of the Atlantic sweep storming on
    their way,
Shining green and silver with the hidden herring
    shoal;
But the Little Waves of Breffny have drenched my
    heart in spray,
And the Little Waves of Breffny go stumbling through
    my soul.

Cois na Teineadh

T. W. Rolleston

Where glows the Irish hearth with peat
There lives a subtle spell—
The faint blue smoke, the gentle heat,
The moorland odours tell.

Of white roads winding by the edge
Of bare, untamèd land,
Where dry stone wall or ragged hedge
Runs wide on either hand.

To cottage lights that lure you in
From rainy Western skies;
And by the friendly glow within
Of simple talk, and wise,

And tales of magic, love or arms
From days when princes met
To listen to the lay that charms
The Connacht peasant yet,

There Honour shines through passions dire,
There beauty blends with mirth—
Wild hearts, ye never did aspire
Wholly for things of earth!

Cold, cold this thousand years—yet still
On many a time-stained page
Your pride, your truth, your dauntless will,
Burn on from age to age.

And still around the fires of peat
Live on the ancient days;
There still do living lips repeat
The old and deathless lays.

And when the wavering wreaths ascend
Blue in the evening air,
The soul of Ireland seems to bend
Above her children there.

Inishail

Anonymous

I will go, and leave the streetways,
    And the world's wild, dinsome places,
With the hurrying, weary feetways,
    And the folks of frenzied faces;
    I will go through darkened spaces,
Morning glad, or starlight pale,
    Through the rivers and the passes,
    Till I find, among the grasses,
    Long sweet sleep among the grasses
Of the graves of Inishail.

Ah, ye daunt me, with your wonder,
    And your toils about you lying,
O ye cities, with your thunder,
    And your children in you, dying,
    And I weary, ever sighing,
For the whisper of the West,
    Where the glow and glamour meeting,
    And the waves on long shores beating,
    Are but echoes of the beating
Of the life's blood in my breast.

I will plait a roof of rashes
    For the low place of my sleeping,
Where the wistful water plashes,
    Crooning, croodling, laughing, weeping,

And the winds from Cruachan sweeping
Join their gladness and their wail;
   Till the angels' glory blinds me,
   And the long sleep comes and finds me,
   In the tangled grasses finds me,
By the graves in Inishail.

The Wind That Shakes the Barley

Katharine Tynan Hinkson

There's music in my heart all day,
   I hear it late and early,
It comes from fields are far away,
   The wind that shakes the barley.
      Ochone!

Above the uplands drenched with dew,
   The sky hangs soft and pearly,
An emerald world is listening to
   The wind that shakes the barley.
      Ochone!

Above the bluest mountain crest
   The lark is singing rarely,
It rocks the singer into rest,
   The wind that shakes the barley.
      Ochone!

Oh, still through summers and through springs
   It calls me late and early.
Come home, come home, come home, it sings,
   The wind that shakes the barley.
          Ochone!

I Have Been to Hy-Brasail

Dora Sigerson Shorter

I have been to Hy-Brasail,
And the Land of Youth have seen,
Much laughter have I heard there,
And birds amongst the green.

Many have I met there,
But no one ever old,
Yet I have left Hy-Brasail
Before my time was told.

Love have I known, too,
As I shall meet no more;
Lost is the magic island,
And I cannot find the shore.

Since I have left Hy-Brasail,
Age has encompassed me,

She plucks me by the shoulder
And will not let me be.

Her face is grey and mournful,
Her hand is hard and cold,
Yet I have left Hy-Brasail
Before my time was told.

The Bells of Shandon

Francis Sylvester Mahoney

With deep affection and recollection
    I often think of the Shandon bells,
Whose sounds so wild would, in days of childhood,
    Fling round my cradle their magic spells—
On this I ponder, where'er I wander,
    And thus grow fonder, sweet Cork, of thee;
            With thy bells of Shandon,
                That sound so grand on
The pleasant waters of the river Lee.

I have heard bells chiming full many a clime in,
    Tolling sublime in cathedral shrine;
While at a glib rate brass tongues would vibrate,
    But all their music spoke nought to thine;
For memory dwelling on each proud swelling

Of thy belfry knelling its bold notes free,
        Made the bells of Shandon
        Sound far more grand on
The pleasant waters of the river Lee.

I have heard bells tolling "old Adrian's mole" in,
    Their thunder rolling from the Vatican,
With cymbals glorious, swinging uproarious
    In the gorgeous turrets of Notre Dame;
But thy sounds were sweeter than the dome of Peter
    Flings o'er the Tiber, pealing solemnly.
        Oh! the bells of Shandon
        Sound far more grand on
The pleasant waters of the river Lee.

There's a bell in Moscow, while on tower and Kiosko,
    In St. Sophia the Turkman gets,
And loud in air, calls men to prayer,
    From the tapering summit of tall minarets.
Such empty phantom I freely grant them,
    But there's an anthem more dear to me,
        It's the bells of Shandon,
        That sound so grand on
The pleasant waters of the river Lee.

A Sigh for Knockmany

William Carleton

Take, proud ambition, take thy fill
    Of pleasures won through toil or crime;
Go, learning, climb thy rugged hill,
    And give thy name to future time:
Philosophy, be keen to see
    Whate'er is just, or false, or vain,
Take each thy meed, but, oh! give me
    To range my mountain glens again.

Pure was the breeze that fann'd my cheek,
    As o'er Knockmany's brow I went;
When every lonely dell could speak
    In airy music, vision sent;
False world, I hate thy cares and thee,
    I hate the treacherous haunts of men;
Give back my early heart to me,
    Give back to me my mountain glen.

How light my youthful visions shone,
    When spann'd by Fancy's radiant form;
But now her glittering bow is gone,
    And leaves me but the cloud and storm.
With wasted form, and cheek all pale—
    With heart long seared by grief and pain;
Dunroe, I'll seek thy native gale,
    I'll tread my mountain glens again.

Thy breeze once more may fan my blood,
    Thy valleys all are lovely still;
And I may stand, where oft I stood,
    In lonely musings on thy hill.
But, ah! the spell is gone;—no art
    In crowded town, or native plain,
Can teach a crush'd and breaking heart
    To pipe the song of youth again.

The Song of Fionnuala

Thomas Moore

Silent, O Moyle, be the roar of thy water,
    Break not, ye breezes, your chain of repose,
While, murmuring mournfully, Lir's lonely daughter
    Tells to the night-star her tale of woes.
When shall the swan, her death-note singing,
    Sleep, with wings in darkness furled?
When will heaven, its sweet bell ringing,
    Call my spirit from this stormy world?

Sadly, O Moyle, to thy winter-wave weeping,
    Fate bids me languish long ages away;
Yet still in her darkness doth Erin lie sleeping,
    Still doth the pure light its dawning delay.

When will that day-star, mildly springing,
    Warm our isle with peace and love?
When will heaven, its sweet bell ringing,
    Call my spirit to the fields above?

A Song of Freedom

Alice Mulligan

In Cavan of little lakes,
    As I was walking with the wind,
And no one seen beside me there,
    There came a song into my mind;
It came as if the whispered voice
    Of one, but none of human kind,
Who walked with me in Cavan then,
    And he invisible as wind.

On Urris of Inish-Owen,
    As I went up the mountain side,
The brook that came leaping down
    Cried to me—for joy it cried;
And when from off the summit far
    I looked o'er land and water wide,
I was more joyous than the brook
    That met me on the mountain side.

To Ara of Connacht's isles,
　　As I went sailing o'er the sea,
The wind's word, the brook's word,
　　The wave's word, was plain to me—
As we are, though she is not,
　　As we are, shall Banba be—
There is no king can rule the wind,
　　There is no fetter for the sea.

Lough Bray

Rose Kavanagh

A little lonely moorland lake,
　　Its waters brown and cool and deep—
The cliff, the hills behind it make
　　A picture for my heart to keep.

For rock and heather, wave and strand,
　　Wore tints I never saw them wear;
The June sunshine was o'er the land,
　　Before, 'twas never half so fair!

The amber ripples sang all day,
　　And singing spilled their crowns of white
Upon the beach, in thin pale spray
　　That streaked the sober sand with light.

The amber ripples sang their song,
    When suddenly from far o'erhead
A lark's pure voice mixed with the throng
    Of lovely things about us spread.

Some flowers were there, so near the brink
    Their shadows in the waves were thrown;
While mosses, green and gray and pink,
    Grew thickly round each smooth dark stone.

And, over all, the summer sky,
    Shut out the town we left behind;
'Twas joy to stand in silence by,
    One bright chain linking mind to mind.

O, little lonely mountain spot!
    Your place within my heart will be
Apart from all Life's busy lot
    A true, sweet, solemn memory.

Killarney

William Larminie

Is there one desires to hear
If within the shores of Eire
Eyes may still behold the scene
Far from Fand's enticements?

Let him seek the southern hills
And those lakes of loveliest water
Where the richest blooms of Spring
Burn to reddest Autumn:
And the clearest echo sings
Notes a goddess taught her.

Ah! 'twas very long ago,
And the words are now denied her:
But the purple hillsides know
Still the tones delightsome,
And their breasts, impassioned, glow
As were Fand beside them.

And though many an isle be fair,
Fairer still is Innisfallen,
Since the hour Cuchullain lay
In the bower enchanted.
See! the ash that waves to-day.
Fand its grandsire planted.

When from wave to mountain-top
All delight thy sense bewilders,
Thou shall own the wonders wrought
Once by her skilled fingers,
Still, though many an age be gone,
Round Killarney lingers.

The Enchanted Island

Luke Aylmer Conolly

To Rathlin's Isle I chanced to sail
  When summer breezes softly blew,
And there I heard so sweet a tale
  That oft I wished it could be true.

They said, at eve, when rude winds sleep,
  And hushed is ev'ry turbid swell,
A mermaid rises from the deep
  And sweetly tunes her magic shell.

And while she plays, rock, dell, and cave,
  In dying falls the sound retain,
As if some choral spirits gave
  Their aid to swell her witching strain.

Then summoned by that dulcet note,
  Uprising to th' admiring view,
A fairy island seems to float
  With tints of many a gorgeous hue.

And glittering fanes, and lofty towers,
  All on this fairy isle are seen:
And waving trees, and shady bowers,
  With more than mortal verdure green.

And as it moves, the western sky
  Glows with a thousand varying rays;
And the calm sea, tinged with each dye,
  Seems like a golden flood of haze.

They also say, if earth or stone
  From verdant Erin's hallowed land
Were on this magic island thrown,
  For ever fixed it then would stand.

But when for this some little boat
  In silence ventures from the shore,
The mermaid sinks—hushed is the note—
  The fairy isle is seen no more.

Beg-Innish

John Millington Synge

Bring Kateen-beug and Maurya Jude
  To dance in Beg-Innish,
And when the lads (they're in Dunquin)
  Have sold their crabs and fish,
Wave fawny shawls and call them in,
And call the little girls who spin,
And seven weavers from Dunquin,
  To dance in Beg-Innish.

I'll play you jigs, and Maurice Kean,
 Where nets are laid to dry,
I've silken strings would draw a dance
 From girls are lame or shy;
Four strings I've brought from Spain and France
To make your long men skip and prance,
Till stars look out to see the dance
 Where nets are laid to dry.

We'll have no priest or peeler in
 To dance in Beg-Innish;
But we'll have drink from M'riarty Jim
 Rowed round while gannets fish,
A keg with porter to the brim,
That every lad may have his whim,
Till we up sails with M'riarty Jim
 And sail from Beg-Innish.

A Dedication

Edmund John Armstrong

My land, my Erin, can we sing of thee
Save in that music ringing through thy vales,
And through thy people's hearts,—how bold and free,

How sadly like a Rachel's piteous wails,
Dying in anguish, faintly, brokenly,
With more of woe than all a poet's tales?

Thy music is thy speech: so half in fear
I link this story now in rhythmic law,
And miss in words that plaintive warble, clear

And dreamful, which first woke my soul with awe,
And thrilled it into motion, as a mere
Is rippled weirdly by the mountain flaw.

Hills o' My Heart

Ethna Carbery

Hills o' my heart!
I have come to you at calling of my one love and only,
   I have left behind the cruel scarlet wind of the
      east,
The hearth of my fathers wanting me is lonely,
   And empty is the place I filled at gathering of
      the feast.

Hills o' my heart!
You have cradled him I love in your green quiet
   hollows,

Your wavering winds have hushed him to soft
    forgetful sleep,
Below dusk boughs where bird-voice after bird-voice
    follows
    In shafts of silver melody that split the hearkening
      deep.

        Hills o' my heart!
Let the herdsman who walks in your high haunted
    places
    Give him strength and courage, and weave his
      dreams alway:
Let your cairn-heaped hero-dead reveal their grand
    exultant faces,
    And the Gentle Folk be good to him betwixt the
      dark and day.

        Hills o' my heart!
And I would the Green Harper might wake his soul
    to singing,
    With music of the golden wires heard when the
      world was new,
That from his lips an echo of its sweetness may
    come ringing,
    A song of pure and noble hopes—a song of all
      things true.

        Hills o' my heart!
For sake of the yellow head that drew me wandering
    over

Your misty crests from my own home where
    sorrow bided then,
I set my seven blessings on your kindly heather
    cover,
    On every starry moorland loch, and every
      shadowy glen.
              Hills o' my heart!

Ireland

Stephen Lucius Gwynn

Ireland, oh Ireland! centre of my longings,
    Country of my fathers, home of my heart!
Overseas you call me: "Why an exile from me?
    Wherefore sea-severed, long leagues apart?"

As the shining salmon, homeless in the sea depths,
    Hear the river call him, scents out the land
Leaps and rejoices in the meeting of the waters,
    Breasts weir and torrent, nests in the sand,

Lives there and loves; yet with the year's returning,
    Rusting in the river, pines for the sea,
Sweeps back again to the ripple of the tideway,
    Roamer of the waters, vagabond and free.

Wanderer am I like the salmon of thy rivers;
    London is my ocean, murmurous and deep,
Tossing and vast; yet through the roar of London
    Comes to me thy summons, calls me in sleep.

Pearly are the skies in the country of my fathers,
    Purple are thy mountains, home of my heart.
Mother of my yearning, love of all my longings,
    Keep me in remembrance, long leagues apart.

THE LORE

The Three Woes

Aubrey de Vere

That angel whose charge was Eiré sang thus, o'er the
    dark Isle winging;
By a virgin his song was heard at a tempest's ruinous
    close:
"Three golden ages God gave while your tender green
    blade was springing;
Faith's earliest harvest is reaped. To-day God sends
    you three woes.

"For ages three without laws ye shall flee as beasts in
    the forest;
For an age and a half age faith shall bring, not peace,
    but a sword;
Then laws shall rend you, like eagles sharp-fanged,
    of your scourges the sorest;
When these three woes are past, look up, for your
    hope is restored.

"The times of your woes shall be twice the time of
    your foregone glory;
But fourfold at last shall lie the grain on your granary
    floor.
The seas in vapour shall flee, and in ashes the
    mountains hoary;
Let God do that which He wills. Let his servants
    endure and adore!"

The Children of Lir

Katharine Tynan Hinkson

Out upon the sand-dunes thrive the coarse long
    grasses,
  Herons standing knee-deep in the brackish pool,
Overhead the sunset fire and flame amasses,
  And the moon to Eastward rises pale and cool:
Rose and green around her, silver-grey and pearly,
  Chequered with the black rooks flying home to bed;
For, to wake at daybreak birds must couch them early,
  And the day's a long one since the dawn was red.

On the chilly lakelet, in that pleasant gloaming,
  See the sad swans sailing: they shall have no rest:
Never a voice to greet them save the bittern's booming
  Where the ghostly sallows sway against the West.
"Sister," saith the grey swan, "Sister, I am weary,"
  Turning to the white swan wet, despairing eyes;
"O," she saith, "my young one." "O," she saith, "my
    dearie,"
  Casts her wings about him with a storm of cries.

Woe for Lir's sweet children whom their vile step-
    mother
  Glamoured with her witch-spells for a thousand
    years;
Died their father raving—on his throne another—
  Blind before the end came from his burning tears.

She—the fiends possess her, torture her for ever,
 Gone is all the glory of the race of Lir;
Gone and long-forgotten like a dream of fever:
 But the swans remember all the days that were.

Hugh, the black and white swan with the beauteous
  feathers;
 Fiachra, the black swan with the emerald breast;
Conn, the youngest, dearest, sheltered in all weathers,
 Him his snow-white sister loves the tenderest.
These her mother gave her as she lay a-dying,
 To her faithful keeping, faithful hath she been,
With her wings spread o'er them when the tempest's
  crying,
 And her songs so hopeful when the sky's serene.

Other swans have nests made 'mid the reeds and
  rushes,
 Lined with downy feathers where the cygnets
  sleep
Dreaming, if a bird dreams, till the daylight blushes,
 Then they sail out swiftly on the current deep,
With the proud swan-father, tall, and strong, and
  stately,
 And the mild swan-mother, grave with household
  cares,
All well-born and comely, all rejoicing greatly:
 Full of honest pleasure is a life like theirs.

A Lamentation

FOR THE DEATH OF SIR MAURICE FITZGERALD, KNIGHT,
OF KERRY, WHO WAS KILLED IN FLANDERS, 1642

James Clarence Mangan (Translator)

There was lifted up one voice of woe,
    One lament of more than mortal grief,
Through the wide South to and fro,
    For a fallen Chief.
In the dead of night that cry thrilled through me,
    I looked out upon the midnight air!
My own soul was all as gloomy,
    As I knelt in prayer.

O'er Loch Gur, that night, once—twice—yea, thrice—
    Passed a wail of anguish for the Brave
That half curled into ice
    Its moon-mirroring wave.
Then uprose a many-toned wild hymn in
    Choral swell from Ogra's dark ravine,
And Mogeely's Phantom Women
    Mourned the Geraldine!

Far on Carah Mona's emerald plains
    Shrieks and sighs were blended many hours.
And Fermoy in fitful strains
    Answered from her towers.
Youghal, Keenalmeaky, Eemokilly,
    Mourned in concert, and their piercing keen

Woke to wondering life the stilly
  Glens of Inchiqueen.

From Loughmoe to yellow Dunanore
  There was fear; the traders of Tralee
Gathered up their golden store,
  And prepared to flee;
For, in ship and hall from night till morning,
  Showed the first faint beamings of the sun,
All the foreigners heard the warning
  Of the Dreaded One!

"This," they spake, "portendeth death to us,
  If we fly not swiftly from our fate!"
Self-conceited idiots! thus
  Ravingly to prate!
Not for base-born higgling Saxon trucksters
  Ring laments like those by shore and sea!
Not for churls with souls like hucksters
  Waileth our Banshee!

For the high Milesian race alone
  Ever flows the music of her woe!
For slain heir to bygone throne,
  And for Chief laid low!
Hark! . . . Again, methinks, I hear her weeping
  Yonder! Is she near me now, as then?
Or was but the night-wind sweeping
  Down the hollow glen?

The Fairies

William Allingham

Up the airy mountain,
　　Down the rushy glen,
We daren't go a-hunting
　　For fear of little men;
Wee folk, good folk,
　　Trooping all together;
Green jacket, red cap,
　　And white owl's feather!

Down along the rocky shore
　　Some make their home,
They live on crispy pancakes
　　Of yellow tide foam;
Some in the reeds
　　Of the black mountain lake,
With frogs for their watch-dogs,
　　All night awake.

High on the hill-top
　　The old King sits;
He is now so old and grey
　　He's nigh lost his wits.
With a bridge of white mist
　　Columbkill he crosses,
On his stately journeys
　　From Slieveleague to Rosses;

Or going up with music
 On cold starry nights,
To sup with the queen
 Of the gay Northern Lights.

They stole little Bridget
 For seven years long;
When she came down again
 Her friends were all gone.
They took her lightly back,
 Between the night and morrow,
They thought that she was fast asleep,
 But she was dead with sorrow.
They have kept her ever since
 Deep within the lake,
On a bed of flag-leaves,
 Watching till she wake.

By the craggy hill-side,
 Through the mosses bare,
They have planted thorn-trees
 For pleasure here and there.
Is any man so daring
 As dig them up in spite,
He shall find their sharpest thorns
 In his bed at night.

Up the airy mountain,
 Down the rushy glen,
We daren't go a-hunting

For fear of little men;
Wee folk, good folk,
    Trooping all together;
Green jacket, red cap,
    And white owl's feather!

The Fairy Well of Lagnanay

Samuel Ferguson

Mournfully, sing mournfully—
    "O listen, Ellen, sister dear;
Is there no help at all for me,
    But only ceaseless sigh and tear?
    Why did not he who left me here,
With stolen hope steal memory?
    O listen, Ellen, sister dear,
(Mournfully, sing mournfully)—
    I'll go away to Sleamish hill,
I'll pluck the fairy hawthorn-tree,
    And let the spirits work their will;
    I care not if for good or ill,
So they but lay the memory
    Which all my heart is haunting still!
(Mournfully, sing mournfully)—
    The Fairies are a silent race,

And pale as lily flowers to see;
   I care not for a blanched face,
   For wandering in a dreaming place,
So I but banish memory:—
   I wish I were with Anna Grace!"
Mournfully, sing mournfully!

Hearken to my tale of woe—
   'Twas thus to weeping Ellen Con,
Her sister said in accents low,
   Her only sister, Una bawn:
   'Twas in their bed before the dawn,
And Ellen answered sad and slow,—
   "Oh Una, Una, be not drawn
(Hearken to my tale of woe)—
   To this unholy grief I pray,
Which makes me sick at heart to know,
   And I will help you if I may:
   —The Fairy Well of Lagnanay—
Lie nearer me, I tremble so,—
   Una, I've heard wise women say
(Hearken to my tale of woe)—
   That if before the dews arise,
True maiden in its icy flow
   With pure hand bathe her bosom thrice,
   Three lady-brackens pluck likewise,
And three times round the fountain go,
   She straight forgets her tears and sighs."
Hearken to my tale of woe!

All, alas! and well-away!
   "Oh, sister Ellen, sister sweet,
Come with me to the hill I pray,
   And I will prove that blessed freet!"
   They rose with soft and silent feet,
They left their mother where she lay,
   Their mother and her care discreet,
(All, alas! and well-away!)
   And soon they reached the Fairy Well,
The mountain's eye, clear, cold, and grey,
   Wide open in the dreary fell:
   How long they stood 'twere vain to tell,
At last upon the point of day,
   Bawn Una bares her bosom's swell,
(All, alas! and well-away!)
   Thrice o'er her shrinking breasts she laves
The gliding glance that will not stay
   Of subtly-streaming fairy waves:—
   And now the charm three brackens craves,
She plucks them in their fring'd array:—
   Now round the well her fate she braves,
All, alas! and well-away!

Save us all from Fairy thrall!
   Ellen sees her face the rim
Twice and thrice, and that is all—
   Fount and hill and maiden swim
   All together melting dim!
"Una! Una!" thou may'st call,
   Sister sad! but lith or limb

(Save us all from Fairy thrall!)
   Never again of Una bawn,
Where now she walks in dreamy hall,
   Shall eye of mortal look upon!
   Oh! can it be the guard was gone,
The better guard than shield or wall?
   Who knows on earth save Jurlagh Daune?
(Save us all from Fairy thrall!)
   Behold the banks are green and bare,
No pit is here within to fall:
   Aye—at the fount you well may stare,
   But nought save pebbles smooth is there,
And small straws twirling one and all.
   Hie thee home, and be thy pray'r,
Save us all from Fairy thrall.

The Stolen Child

William Butler Yeats

Where dips the rocky highland
   Of Sleuth Wood in the lake,
There lies a leafy island
   Where flapping herons wake
The drowsy water-rats.
There we've hid our fairy vats
Full of berries,

And of reddest stolen cherries.
Come away, O, human child!
To the woods and waters wild,
With a fairy hand in hand,
For the world's more full of weeping than
            you can understand.

Where the wave of moonlight glosses
    The dim grey sands with light,
Far off by furthest Rosses
    We foot it all the night,
Weaving olden dances,
Mingling hands, and mingling glances,
    Till the moon has taken flight;
To and fro we leap,
    And chase the frothy bubbles,
    While the world is full of troubles.
And is anxious in its sleep.
Come away! O, human child!
To the woods and waters wild,
With a fairy hand in hand,
For the world's more full of weeping than
            you can understand.

Where the wandering water gushes
    From the hills above Glen-Car,
In pools among the rushes,
    That scarce could bathe a star,
We seek for slumbering trout,

And whispering in their ears;
    We give them evil dreams,
Leaning softly out
    From ferns that drop their tears
        Of dew on the young streams.
Come! O, human child!
To the woods and waters wild,
With a fairy hand in hand,
For the world's more full of weeping than
        you can understand.

Away with us, he's going,
    The solemn-eyed;
He'll hear no more the lowing
    Of the calves on the warm hill-side.
Or the kettle on the hob
    Sing peace into his breast;
Or see the brown mice bob
    Round and round the oatmeal chest.
For he comes, the human child,
To the woods and waters wild,
With a fairy hand in hand,
For the world's more full of weeping than
        he can understand.

How Oft Has the Banshee Cried

Thomas Moore

How oft has the Banshee cried!
How oft has death untied
Bright links that Glory wove,
Sweet bonds entwined by Love!
Peace to each manly soul that sleepeth;
Rest to each faithful eye that weepeth;
Long may the fair and brave
Sigh o'er the hero's grave!

We're fallen on evil days!
Star after star decays,
Every bright name that shed
Light o'er the land is fled.
Dark falls the tear of him that mourneth
Lost joy, or hope that ne'er returneth:
But brightly flows the tear
Wept o'er a hero's bier.

Quenched are our beacon lights—
Thou, of the Hundred Fights!
Thou, on whose burning tongue
Truth, peace and freedom hung!
Both mute—but long as valor shineth,
Or mercy's soul at war repineth,
So long shall Erin's pride
Tell how they lived and died.

Over the Hills and Far Away

(To E. Nesbit)

Nora Chesson

Last night, last night, in the dark o' the moon
Into my dreams slid a faery tune . . .
It slew the dreams that I dreamed of him,
With its moonshine music, faint and dim.
What tune should the fairy pipers play
But "Over the Hills and Far Away?"

The music called to my idle feet,
And O! the music was wild and sweet:
I left my dreams and my lonely bed,
And followed afar where the music led—
And never a tune did the pipers play
But "Over the Hills and Far Away."

Over the hills and far away,
What love has tenderer words to say?
Love that lifteth or bows the head,
Love that liveth or love that's dead?
Hills that are far away are fair,
And I followed the ghost of my lover there.

We danced all night in a silent band,
I and my lover, hand in hand:
We danced, nor knew till the dew was dry
That deep slept Donat and lone slept I—

We took no thought of the coming day
Over the hills and far away.

My eyes are blind with the growing light,
And O my grief! that the day was night—
For my heart is broke, for my lover's eyes,
And all day long in my ears there cries
The tune of the fairy pipes that play
"Over the Hills and Far Away."

The Fairy Nurse

Edward Walsh

Sweet babe! a golden cradle holds thee,
And soft the snow-white fleece enfolds thee;
In airy bower I'll watch thy sleeping,
Where branchy trees to the breeze are sweeping.
            Shuheen sho, lulo lo

When mothers languish broken-hearted,
When young wives are from husbands parted,
Ah! little think the keeners lonely,
They weep some time-worn fairy only.
            Shuheen sho, lulo lo!

Within our magic halls of brightness,
Trips many a foot of snowy whiteness;
Stolen maidens, queens of fairy—
And kings and chiefs a sluagh shee airy.
        Shuheen sho, lulo lo!

Rest thee, babe! I love thee dearly,
And as thy mortal mother nearly;
Ours is the swiftest steed and proudest,
That moves where the tramp of the host is loudest.
        Shuheen sho, lulo lo!

Rest thee, babe! for soon thy slumbers
Shall flee at the magic koelshie's numbers;
In airy bower I'll watch thy sleeping,
Where branchy trees to the breeze are sweeping.
        Shuheen sho, lulo lo!

The Green Little Shamrock of Ireland
Andrew Cherry

There's a dear little plant that grows in our isle,
   'Twas St. Patrick himself sure that set it;
And the sun on his labour with pleasure did smile,
   And with dew from his eye often wet it.

It thrives through the bog, through the brake, and
    the mireland;
And he called it the dear little shamrock of Ireland—
    The sweet little shamrock, the dear little
      shamrock,
    The sweet little, green little, shamrock of Ireland!

This dear little plant still grows in our land,
    Fresh and fair as the daughters of Erin,
Whose smiles can bewitch, whose eyes can command,
    In each climate that they may appear in;
And shine through the bog, through the brake, and
    the mireland,
Just like their own dear little shamrock of Ireland.
    The sweet little shamrock, the dear little shamrock,
    The sweet little, green little, shamrock of Ireland!

This dear little plant that springs from our soil,
    When its three little leaves are extended,
Denotes on one stalk we together should toil,
    And ourselves by ourselves be befriended;
And still through the bog, through the brake, and
    the mireland,
From one root should branch, like the shamrock
    of Ireland.
    The sweet little shamrock, the dear little shamrock,
    The sweet little, green little, shamrock of Ireland!

The Spell-Struck

T. W. Rolleston

She walks as she were moving
   Some mystic dance to tread,
So falls her gliding footstep,
   So leans her listening head;

For once to fairy harping
   She danced upon the hill,
And through her brain and bosom
   The music pulses still.

Her eyes are bright and tearless,
   But wide with yearning pain;
She longs for nothing earthly,
   But O! to hear again

The sound that held her listening
   Upon her moonlit path!
The rippling fairy music
   That filled the lonely rath.

Her lips, that once have tasted
   The fairy banquet's bliss,
Shall glad no mortal lover
   With maiden smile or kiss.

She's dead to all things living
  Since that November Eve;
And when she dies in autumn
  No living thing will grieve.

The Fairy Thorn

Samuel Ferguson

"Get up, our Anna dear, from the weary spinning-wheel;
For your father's on the hill, and your mother is
      asleep;
Come up above the crags, and we'll dance a
      Highland reel
Around the Fairy Thorn on the steep."

At Anna Grace's door 'twas thus the maidens cried,
Three merry maidens fair in kirtles of the green;
And Anna laid the rock and the weary wheel aside,
The fairest of the four, I ween.

They're glancing through the glimmer of the quiet
      eve,
Away in milky wavings of neck and ankle bare;
The heavy-sliding stream in its sleepy song they leave,
And the crags in the ghostly air.

And linking hand-in-hand, and singing as they go,
The maids along the hillside have ta'en their fearless
     way,
Till they come to where the rowan trees in lonely
     beauty grow
Beside the Fairy Hawthorn grey.

The Hawthorn stands between the ashes tall and slim,
Like matron with her twin grand-daughters at her
     knee;
The rowan berries cluster o'er her low head grey
     and dim
In ruddy kisses sweet to see.

The merry maidens four have ranged them in a row,
Between each lovely couple a stately rowan stem,
And away in mazes wavy, like skimming birds they go,
Oh, never carolled bird like them!

But solemn is the silence on the silvery haze
That drinks away their voices in echoless repose,
And dreamily the evening has stilled the haunted braes,
And dreamier the gloaming grows.

And sinking one by one, like lark-notes from the sky,
When the falcon's shadow saileth across the open shaw,
Are hushed the maidens' voices, as cowering down
     they lie
In the flutter of their sudden awe.

For, from the air above and the grassy ground
    beneath,
And from the mountain-ashes and the old white-
    thorn between,
A power of faint enchantment doth through their
    beings breathe,
And they sink down together on the green.

They sink together silent, and stealing side to side,
They fling their lovely arms o'er their drooping
    necks so fair,
Then vainly strive again their naked arms to hide,
For their shrinking necks again are bare.

Thus clasped and prostrate all, with their heads
    together bowed,
Soft o'er their bosoms beating—the only human
    sound—
They hear the silky footsteps of the silent fairy crowd,
Like a river in the air gliding round.

Nor scream can any raise, nor prayer can any say,
But wild, wild the terror of the speechless three—
For they feel fair Anna Grace drawn silently away,
By whom they dare not look to see.

They feel their tresses twine with her parting locks
    of gold,
And the curls elastic falling, as her head withdraws.

They feel her sliding arms from their trancéd arms
     unfold,
But they dare not look to see the cause;

For heavy on their senses the faint enchantment lies
Through all that night of anguish and perilous
     amaze
And neither fear nor wonder can ope their quivering
     eyes,
Or their limbs from the cold ground raise;

Till out of night the earth has rolled her dewy side,
With every haunted mountain and streamy vale
     below;
When, as the mist dissolves in the yellow
     morningtide,
The maidens' trance dissolveth so.

Then fly the ghastly three as swiftly as they may,
And tell their tale of sorrow to anxious friends in
     vain—
They pined away and died within the year and day,
And ne'er was Anna Grace seen again.

The Warnings

Alice Furlong

I was milking in the meadow when I heard the
    Banshee keening:
Little birds were in the nest, lambs were on the lea,
Upon the brow o' the Fairy-hill a round gold moon
    was leaning—
She parted from the esker as the Banshee keened
    for me.

I was weaving by the door-post, when I heard the
    Death-watch beating:
And I signed the Cross upon me, and I spoke the
    Name of Three.
High and fair, through cloud and air, a silver moon
    was fleeting—
But the night began to darken as the Death-watch
    beat for me.

I was sleepless on my pillow when I heard the Dead
    man calling,
The Dead man that lies drowned at the bottom of
    the sea.
Down in the West, in wind and mist, a dim white
    moon was falling—
Now must I rise and go to him, the Dead who calls
    on me.

The Love-Talker

Ethna Carbery

I met the Love-Talker one eve in the glen,
He was handsomer than any of our handsome young
    men,
His eyes were blacker than the sloe, his voice sweeter
    far
Than the crooning of old Kevin's pipes beyond in
    Coolnagar.

I was bound for the milking with a heart fair and free—
My grief! my grief! that bitter hour drained the life
    from me;
I thought him human lover, though his lips on mine
    were cold,
And the breath of death blew keen on me within his
    hold.

I know not what way he came, no shadow fell behind,
But all the sighing rushes swayed beneath a faery wind
The thrush ceased its singing, a mist crept about,
We two clung together—with the world shut out.

Beyond the ghostly mist I could hear my cattle low,
The little cow from Ballina, clean as driven snow,
The dun cow from Kerry, the roan from Inisheer,
Oh, pitiful their calling—and his whispers in my ear!

His eyes were a fire; his words were a snare;
I cried my mother's name, but no help was there;
I made the blessed Sign; then he gave a dreary moan,
A wisp of cloud went floating by, and I stood alone.

Running ever through my head, is an old-time rune—
"Who meets the Love-Talker must weave her shroud
    soon."
My mother's face is furrowed with the salt tears that fall,
But the kind eyes of my father are the saddest sight
    of all.

I have spun the fleecy lint, and now my wheel is still,
The linen length is woven for my shroud fine and
    chill,
I shall stretch me on the bed where a happy maid I
    lay—
Pray for the soul of Mairé Og at dawning of the day!

Song of the Ghost

Alfred Percival Graves

When all were dreaming
    But Pastheen Power,
A light came streaming
    Beneath her bower:

A heavy foot
    At her door delayed,
A heavy hand
    On the latch was laid.

"Now who dare venture,
    At this dark hour,
Unbid to enter
    My maiden bower?"
"Dear Pastheen, open
    The door to me,
And your true lover
    You'll surely see."

"My own true lover,
    So tall and brave,
Lives exiled over
    The angry wave."
"Your true love's body
    Lies on the bier,
His faithful spirit
    Is with you here."

"His look was cheerful,
    His voice was gay;
Your speech is fearful,
    Your face is grey;
And sad and sunken
    Your eye of blue,

But Patrick, Patrick,
    Alas! 'tis you!"

Ere dawn was breaking
    She heard below
The two cocks shaking
    Their wings to crow.
"Oh, hush you, hush you,
    Both red and grey,
Or you will hurry
    My love away.

"Oh, hush your crowing,
    Both grey and red,
Or he'll be going
    To join the dead;
Or, cease from calling
    His ghost to the mould,
And I'll come crowning
    Your combs with gold."

When all were dreaming
    But Pastheen Power,
A light went streaming
    From out her bower;
And on the morrow,
    When they awoke,
They knew that sorrow
    Her heart had broke.

The Others

Seumas O'Sullivan

From our hidden places
   By a secret path,
We come in the moonlight
   To the side of the green rath.

There the night through
   We take our pleasure,
Dancing to such a measure
   As earth never knew.

To song and dance
   And lilt without a name,
So sweetly breathed
   'Twould put a bird to shame.

And many a young maiden
   Is there, of mortal birth,
Her young eyes laden
   With dreams of earth.

And many a youth entranced
   Moves slowly in the wildered round,
His brave lost feet enchanted,
   With the rhythm of faery sound.

Music so forest wild
    And piercing sweet would bring
Silence on blackbirds singing
    Their best in the ear of spring.

And now they pause in their dancing,
    And look with troubled eyes,
Earth straying children
    With sudden memory wise.

They pause, and their eyes in the moonlight
    With fairy wisdom cold,
Grow dim and a thought goes fluttering
    In the hearts no longer old.

And then the dream forsakes them,
    And sighing, they turn anew,
As the whispering music takes them,
    To the dance of the elfin crew.

O many a thrush and a blackbird
    Would fall to the dewy ground,
And pine away in silence
    For envy of such a sound.

So the night through
    In our sad pleasure,
We dance to many a measure,
    That earth never knew.

The Shadow People

Francis Ledwidge

Old lame Bridget doesn't hear
Fairy music in the grass
When the gloaming's on the mere
And the shadow people pass:
Never hears their slow, grey feet
Coming from the village street
Just beyond the parson's wall,
Where the clover globes are sweet
And the mushroom's parasol
Opens in the moonlit rain.
Every night I hear them call
From their long and merry train.
Old lame Bridget says to me,
"It's just your fancy, child."
She cannot believe I see
Laughing faces in the wild,
Hands that twinkle in the sedge
Where the finny minnows quiver,
Shaping on a blue wave's ledge
Bubble foam to sail the river.
And the sunny hands to me
Beckon ever, beckon ever.
Oh! I would be wild and free
And with the shadow people be.

The Faerie's Child

Thomas Caulfield Irwin

Amid the nut grove, still and brown,
　　The Faerie's Child is walking.
List, list, as the leaves come down,
　　To the sprites around her talking.
　　　　Along the windy, waving grass
　　　　　　Their evening whispers breathe and pass:
　　　　　　From yon aged bending bough
　　　　　　Their leafy language floats below;
And now o'erhead in the air 'tis streaming.
　　Oh! who can tell what things she hears—
　　What secrets of the faery spheres,
　　That fill her eyes with silent tears!
Sweet wandering fancy-charmed child,
With cheek so pale, and eyes so wild.
Oh! what shall come of this lonely dreaming!

Down by the sun-dry harvest road,
　　Through quiet evening's hours,
She paces with her scented load
　　Of late-year moss and flowers.
　　　　Blooms from the wood of every hue,
　　　　　　Moon pale, purple, jet, and blue;
　　　　　　Woven in bunches, and lightly press'd
　　　　　　Upon her simple, snowy breast,
　　　　　　And through the brown locks wildly tressed
　　Nodding in crownlets o'er her.

And, lo! as the cloud on ocean's brim
With moonlight has enriched its rim,
A quaint wild shape, with kindly eyes,
And a smile like a star of the distant skies,
Goes tripping along the path before her.

Now by her pillow, small and white,
    'Mid faded leaflets lying,
An eager star, like a taper light,
    O'er the curtain's edge is spying.
        The scent of the broom-buds fills the room;
        The window is full of the bare blue gloom,
        And by the low hearth ashily sinking,
        Half asleep is the faery winking.
        Out in the air there comes a sound
        Of music eddying round and round
        The ivied chimneys—swooning near
        The glassy pane, and streaming clear
        As moonlight into the little ear,
    Like a shell in brown weed gleaming;
        And, just as the first bird, mounted high
        On the sycamore's tinkling canopy,
        Sings to the first red streak of day,
        Her soul with the faeries speeds away,
        O'er field, and stream, and hamlet grey,
    Where the weary folk are dreaming.

The Fairy Music

Nora Hopper

There's many feet on the moor to-night, and they
    fall so light as they turn and pass,
So light and true that they shake no dew from the
    featherfew and the hungry grass.
I drank no sup and I broke no crumb of their food,
    but dumb at their feast sat I;
For their dancing feet and their piping sweet, now I
    sit and greet till I'm like to die.

Oh kind, kind folk, to the words you spoke I shut my
    ears and I would not hear!
And now all day what my own kin say falls sad and
    strange on my careless ear;
For I'm listening, listening, all day long to a fairy song
    that is blown to me,
Over the broom and the canna's bloom, and I know
    the doom of the Ceol-Sidhe.

I take no care now for bee or bird, for a voice I've
    heard that is sweeter yet.
My wheel stands idle: at death or bridal apart I stand
    and my prayers forget.
When Ulick speaks of my wild-rose cheeks, and his
    kind love seeks out my heart that's cold,
I take no care though he speaks me fair, for the new
    love casts out the love that's cold.

I take no care for the blessed prayer, for my mother's
    hand or my mother's call.
There ever rings in my ear and sings, a voice more
    dear and more sweet than all.
Cold, cold's my breast, and broke's my rest, and oh
    it's blest to be dead I'd be,
Held safe and fast from the fairy blast, and deaf at
    last to the Ceol-Sidhe!

The Banshee

John Todhunter

Green, in the wizard arms,
Of the foam-bearded Atlantic,
An isle of old enchantment,
A melancholy isle,
Enchanted and dreaming lies;
And there, by Shannon's flowing,
In the moonlight, spectre thin,
The spectre Erin sits.

An aged desolation
She sits by old Shannon's flowing,
A mother of many children,
Of children exiled and dead,
In her home, with bent head, homeless,

Clasping her knees she sits,
Keening, keening!
And at her keene the fairy-grass
Trembles on dun and barrow;
Around the foot of her ancient crosses
The grave-grass shakes and the nettle swings;
In haunted glens the meadow-sweet
Flings to the night-wind
Her mystic mournful perfume;
The sad spearmint by holy wells
Breathes melancholy balm.

Sometimes she lifts her head,
With blue eyes tearless,
And gazes athwart the reek of night
Upon things long past,
Upon things to come.

And sometimes, when the moon
Brings tempest upon the deep,
And roused Atlantic thunders from his caverns in
     the West,
The wolf-hound at her feet
Springs up with a mighty bay,
And chords of mystery sound from the wild harp at
     her side,
Strung from the heart of poets;
And she flies on the verge of the tempest
Around her shuddering isle,
With grey hair streaming:

A meteor of evil omen,
The spectre of hope forlorn,
Keening, keening!

She keenes, and the strings of her wild harp shiver
On the gusts of night:
O'er the four waters she keenes—over Moyle she
   keenes,
O'er the Sea of Milith, and the Strait of
   Strongbow,
And the Ocean of Columbus.

And the Fianna hear, and the ghosts of her cloudy
   hovering heroes;
And the swan, Fianoula, wails o'er the waters of
   Inisfail,
Chanting her song of destiny,
The rune of the weaving Fates.

And the nations hear in the void and quaking time
   of night,
Sad unto dawning, dirges,
Solemn dirges,
And snatches of bardic song;
Their souls quake in the void and quaking time of
   night,
And they dream of the weird of kings,
And tyrannies moulting, sick
In the dreadful wind of change.

Wail no more, lonely one, mother of exiles, wail
   no more,
Banshee of the world—no more!
Thy sorrows are the world's, thou art no more alone;
Thy wrongs, the world's.

The Geraldine's Daughter

Anonymous

Speak low!—speak low—the banshee is crying;
Hark! hark to the echo!—she's dying! "she's dying."
What shadow flits dark'ning the face of the water?
'Tis the swan of the lake—'tis *the Geraldine's Daughter.*

Hush, hush! have you heard what the banshee said?
O! list to the echo! she's dead! "she's dead!"
No shadow now dims the face of the water;
Gone, gone is the wraith of *the Geraldine's Daughter.*

The step of yon train is heavy and slow,
There's wringing of hands, there's breathing of woe;
What melody rolls over mountain and water?
'Tis the funeral chant of *the Geraldine's Daughter.*

The requiem sounds like the plaintive moan
Which the wind makes over the sepulchre's stone;

"O, why did she die? our hearts' blood had bought her!
O, why did she die, *the Geraldine's Daughter*?"

The thistle-beard floats—the wild roses wave
With the blast that sweeps over the newly-made grave;
The stars dimly twinkle, and hoarse falls the water,
While night-birds are wailing *the Geraldine's Daughter*.

The Lepracaun; or, Fairy Shoemaker
William Allingham

I
Little Cowboy, what have you heard,
 Up on the lonely rath's green mound?
Only the plaintive yellow bird
 Sighing in sultry fields around,
Chary, chary, chary, chee-ee!—
Only the grasshopper and the bee?—
   "Tip tap, rip-rap,
    Tick-a-tack-too!
  Scarlet leather, sewn together,
   This will make a shoe.
  Left, right, pull it tight;
   Summer days are warm;
  Underground in winter,
   Laughing at the storm!"
Lay your ear close to the hill.

Do you not catch the tiny clamour,
Busy click of an elfin hammer,
Voice of the Lepracaun singing shrill
　　As he merrily plies his trade?
　　　He's a span
　　　And a quarter in height.
Get him in sight, hold him tight,
　　　And you're a made
　　　　Man!

II

You watch your cattle the summer day,
Sup on potatoes, sleep in the hay;
　　How would you like to roll in your carriage,
　　Look for a duchess's daughter in marriage?
Seize the Shoemaker—then you may!
　　　"Big boots a-hunting,
　　　Sandals in the hall,
　　White for a wedding-feast,
　　　Pink for a ball.
　　This way, that way,
　　　So we make a shoe;
　　Getting rich every stitch,
　　　Tick-tack-too!"
Nine-and-ninety treasure-crocks
This keen miser-fairy hath,
Hid in mountains, woods, and rocks,
Ruin and round-tow'r, cave and rath,
　　And where the cormorants build;
　　　From times of old

Guarded by him;
Each of them fill'd
Full to the brim
With gold!

III

I caught him at work one day, myself,
In the castle-ditch, where foxglove grows,—
A wrinkled, wizen'd, and bearded Elf,
Spectacles stuck on his pointed nose,
Silver buckles to his hose,
Leather apron—shoe in his lap—
"Rip-rap, tip-tap,
Tick-tack-too!
(A grasshopper on my cap!
Away the moth flew!)
Buskins for a fairy prince,
Brogues for his son,—
Pay me well, pay me well,
When the job is done!"
The rogue was mine, beyond a doubt.
I stared at him; he stared at me;
"Servant, Sir!" "Humph!" says he,
And pull'd a snuff-box out.
He took a long pinch, look'd better pleased,
The queer little Lepracaun;
Offer'd the box with a whimsical grace,—
Pouf! he flung the dust in my face,
And, while I sneezed,
Was gone!

The Song of Wandering Ængus

William Butler Yeats

I went out to the hazel wood,
    Because a fire was in my head,
And cut and peeled a hazel wand,
    And hooked a berry to a thread;
And when white moths were on the wing,
    And moth-like stars were flickering out,
I dropped the berry in a stream
    And caught a little silver trout.

When I had laid it on the floor
    I went to blow the fire a-flame,
But something rustled on the floor,
    And someone called me by my name:
It had become a glimmering girl
    With apple blossom in her hair
Who called me by my name and ran
    And faded through the brightening air.

Though I am old with wandering
    Through hollow lands and hilly lands,
I will find out where she has gone,
    And kiss her lips and take her hands;
And walk among long dappled grass,
    And pluck till time and times are done
The silver apples of the moon,
    The golden apples of the sun.

THE PEOPLE

The Celts

Thomas D'Arcy McGee

Long, long ago, beyond the misty space
    Of twice a thousand years,
In Erin old there dwelt a mighty race
    Taller than Roman spears;
Like oaks and towers, they had a giant grace,
    Were fleet as deers:
With winds and waves they made their biding-place,
    The Western shepherd seers.

Their ocean-god was *Mananan Mac Lir*,
    Whose angry lips
In their white foam full often would inter
    Whole fleets of ships:
Crom was their day-god, and their thunderer
    Made morning and eclipse:
Bride was their queen of song, and unto her
    They pray'd with fire-touch'd lips.

Great were their acts, their passions, and their sports;
    With clay and stone
They piled on strath and shore those mystic forts,
    Not yet undone;
On cairn-crown'd hills they held their council courts;
    While youths—alone—
With giant-dogs, explored the elks' resorts,
    And brought them down.

Of these was *Finn*, the father of the bard
    Whose ancient song
Over the clamour of all change is heard,
    Sweet-voiced and strong.
Finn once o'ertook Granu, the golden-hair'd,
    The fleet and young:
From her, the lovely, and from him, the feared,
    The primal poet sprung—

Ossian!—two thousand years of mist and change
    Surround thy name;
Thy Finnian heroes now no longer range
    The hills of Fame.
The very name of Finn and Gael sound strange;
    Yet thine the same
By miscall'd lake and desecrated grange
    Remains, and shall remain!

The Druid's altar and the Druid's creed
    We scarce can trace;
There is not left an undisputed deed
    Of all your race—
Save your majestic Song, which hath their speed,
    And strength, and grace:
In that sole song they live, and love, and bleed—
    It bears them on through space.

Inspired giant, shall we e'er behold,
    In our own time,
One fit to speak your spirit on the wold,

Or seize your rhyme?
One pupil of the past, as mighty-soul'd
    As in the prime
Were the fond, fair, and beautiful, and bold—
    They of your song sublime?

The Irishman

James Orr

The savage loves his native shore,
    Though rude the soil and chill the air;
Then well may Erin's sons adore
    Their isle, which Nature formed so fair.
What flood reflects a shore so sweet
    As Shannon great, or pastoral Bann?
Or who a friend or foe can meet
    So generous as an Irishman?

His hand is rash, his heart is warm,
    But honesty is still his guide;
None more repents a deed of harm,
    And none forgives with nobler pride;
He may be duped, but won't be dared—
    More fit to practise than to plan;
He dearly earns his poor reward,
    And spends it like an Irishman.

If strange or poor, for you he'll pay,
    And guide to where you safe may be;
If you're his guest, while e'er you stay
    His cottage holds a jubilee.
His inmost soul he will unlock,
    And if he may your secrets scan,
Your confidence he scorns to mock,
    For faithful is an Irishman.

By honour bound in woe or weal,
    Whate'er she bids he dares to do;
Try him with bribes—they won't prevail;
    Prove him in fire—you'll find him true.
He seeks not safety, let his post
    Be where it ought, in danger's van;
And if the field of fame be lost,
    It won't be by an Irishman.

Erin! loved land! from age to age
    Be thou more great, more famed, and free;
May peace be thine, or, should'st thou wage
    Defensive war, cheap victory.
May plenty bloom in every field
    Which gentle breezes softly fan,
And cheerful smiles serenely gild
    The home of every Irishman!

Ailleen

John Banim

'Tis not for love of gold I go,
   'Tis not for love of fame;
Tho' fortune should her smile bestow
   And I may win a name,
          Ailleen,
   And I may win a name.

And yet it is for gold I go,
   And yet it is for fame,
That they may deck another brow,
   And bless another name,
          Ailleen,
   And bless another name.

For this, but this, I go—for this
   I lose thy love awhile;
And all the soft and quiet bliss
   Of thy young, faithful smile,
          Ailleen,
   Of thy young, faithful smile.

And I go to brave a world I hate,
   And woo it o'er and o'er,
And tempt a wave, and try a fate
   Upon a stranger shore,
          Ailleen,
   Upon a stranger shore.

O! when the bays are all my own,
     I know a heart will care!
O! when the gold is wooed and won,
     I know a brow shall wear,
                Ailleen,
     I know a brow shall wear!

And when with both returned again,
     My native land to see,
I know a smile will meet me there,
     And a hand will welcome me,
                Ailleen,
     And a hand will welcome me!

To the Rose Upon the Rood of Time

William Butler Yeats

Red Rose, proud Rose, sad Rose of all my days!
Come near me, while I sing the ancient ways:
Cuhoollin battling with the bitter tide;
The Druid, gray, wood-nurtured, quiet-eyed,
Who cast round Fergus dreams, and ruin untold;
And thine own sadness, whereof stars, grown old
In dancing silver sandalled on the sea,
Sing in their high and lonely melody.
Come near, that no more blinded by man's fate,
I find under the boughs of love and hate,

In all poor foolish things that live a day,
Eternal beauty wandering on her way.

Come near, come near, come near—Ah, leave me still
A little space for the rose-breath to fill!
Lest I no more hear common things that crave;
The weak worm hiding down in its small cave,
The field mouse running by me in the grass,
And heavy mortal hopes that toil and pass;
But seek alone to hear the strange things said
By God to the bright hearts of those long dead,
And learn to chaunt a tongue men do not know.
Come near; I would, before my time to go,
Sing of old Eire and the ancient ways:
Red Rose, proud Rose, sad Rose of all my days.

The Irish Peasant Girl

Charles Joseph Kickham

She lived beside the Anner,
At the foot of Slievna-man,
A gentle peasant girl,
With mild eyes like the dawn;
Her lips were dewy rosebuds;
Her teeth of pearls rare;
And a snow-drift 'neath a beechen bough
Her neck and nut-brown hair.

How pleasant 'twas to meet her
On Sunday, when the bell
Was filling with its mellow tones
Lone wood and grassy dell
And when at eve young maidens
Strayed the river bank along,
The widow's brown-haired daughter
Was loveliest of the throng.

O brave, brave Irish girls—
We well may call you brave!—
Sure the least of all your perils
Is the stormy ocean wave,
When you leave our quiet valleys,
And cross the Atlantic's foam,
To hoard your hard-won earnings
For the helpless ones at home.

"Write word to my own dear mother—
Say, we'll meet with God above;
And tell my little brothers
I send them all my love;
May the angels ever guard them,
Is their dying sister's prayer"—
And folded in a letter
Was a braid of nut-brown hair.

Ah, cold and well-nigh callous,
This weary heart has grown
For thy helpless fate, dear Ireland,

And for sorrows of my own;
Yet a tear my eye will moisten,
When by Anner side I stray,
For the lily of the mountain foot
That withered far away.

The Wearin' o' the Green

Anonymous

Oh, Paddy dear! and did ye hear the news that's goin'
    round?
The shamrock is forbid by law to grow on Irish ground!
No more St. Patrick's day we'll keep; his colour can't
    be seen,
For there's a cruel law ag'in' the Wearin' o' the Green!

I met with Napper Tandy, and he took me by the hand,
And he said, "How's pour ould Ireland, and how
    does she stand?"
She's the most distressful country that ever yet was
    seen,
For they're hanging men and women there for the
    Wearin' o' the Green.

An' if the colour we must wear is England's cruel red,
Let it remind us of the blood that Ireland has shed;

Then pull the shamrock from your hat, and throw it
   on the sod,
An' never fear, 'twill take root there, though under
   foot 'tis trod.

When law can stop the blades of grass from growin'
   as they grow,
An' when the leaves in summer time their colour dare
   not show,
Then I will change the colour, too, I wear in my
   caubeen;
But till that day, plaise God, I'll stick to the Wearin'
   o' the Green.

The Irish Mother in the Penal Days

John Banim

Now welcome, welcome, baby-boy, unto a mother's
   fears,
The pleasure of her sufferings, the rainbow of her tears,
The object of your father's hope, in all the hopes to do,
A future man of his own land, to live him o'er anew!

How fondly on thy little brow a mother's eye would
   trace,
And in thy little limbs, and in each feature of thy face,

His beauty, worth, and manliness, and everything
    that's his,
Except, my boy, the answering mark of where the
    fetter is!

Oh! many a weary hundred years his sires that fetter
    wore,
And he has worn it since the day that him his mother
    bore;
And now, my son, it waits on you, the moment you
    are born;
The old hereditary badge of suffering and scorn!

Alas, my boy, so beautiful!—alas, my love so brave!
And must your gallant Irish limbs still drag it to the
    grave?
And you, my son, yet have a son, freedom'd a slave
    to be,
Whose mother still must weep o'er him the tears I weep
    o'er thee!

An Exile's Mother

Emily Lawless

There's famine in the land, its grip is tightening still,
There's trouble, black and bitter, on every side I glance,

There are dead upon the roadside, and dead upon
   the hill,
But my Jamie's safe and well away in France,
               Happy France,
In the far-off, gay and gallant land of France.

The sea sobs to the grey shore, the grey shore to the sea.
Men meet and greet, and part again as in some evil
   trance,
There's a bitter blight upon us, as plain as plain can be,
But my Jamie's safe and well away in France,
               Happy France,
In the far-off, gay and gallant land of France.

Oh not for all the coined gold that ever I could name
Would I bring you back, my Jamie, from your song,
   and feast, and dance,
Would I bring you to the hunger, the weariness and
   shame,
Would I bring you back to Clare out of France.
               Happy France,
From the far-off, gay and gallant land of France.

I'm no great sleeper now, for the nights are cruel cold,
And if there be a bit of sup 'tis by some friendly chance,
But I keep my old heart warm, and I keep my
   courage bold
By thinking of my Jamie safe in France,
               Happy France,
In the far-off, gay and gallant land of France.

The Famine Year

Lady Wilde

Weary men, what reap ye?—Golden corn for the
  stranger.
What sow ye?—Human corses that wait for the avenger.
Fainting forms, hunger-stricken, what see ye in the
  offing?—
Stately ships to bear our food away, amid the stranger's
  scoffing.
There's a proud array of soldiers—what do they round
  your door?
They guard our master's granaries from the thin hands
  of the poor.
Pale mothers, wherefore weeping? Would to God that
  we were dead—
Our children swoon before us, and we cannot give
  them bread.

Little children, tears are strange upon your infant
  faces,
God meant you but to smile within your mother's
  soft embraces.
Oh, we know not what is smiling, and we know not
  what is dying;
But we're hungry, very hungry, and we cannot stop
  our crying.
And some of us grow cold and white—we know not
  what it means;

But, as they lie beside us we tremble in our dreams.

There's a gaunt crowd on the highway—are you come
    to pray to man,

With hollow eyes that cannot weep, and for words
    your faces wan?

No; the blood is dead within our veins—we care not
    now for life;

Let us die hid in the ditches, far from children and
    from wife!

We cannot stay and listen to their raving famished
    cries—

Bread! Bread! Bread! and none to still their agonies.

We left our infants playing with their dead mother's
    hand:

We left our maidens maddened by the fever's scorching
    brand:

Better, maiden, thou wert strangled in thy own dark-
    twisted tresses—

Better, infant, thou wert smothered in thy mother's
    first caresses.

We are fainting in our misery, but God will hear our
    groan;

Yet, if fellowmen desert us, will He hearken from His
    throne?

Accursed are we in our own land, yet toil we still and
    toil;

But the stranger reaps our harvest—the alien owns
    our soil.

O Christ! how have we sinned, that on our native plains
We perish homeless, naked, starved, with branded
    brow like Cain's?
Dying, dying wearily, with a torture sure and slow—
Dying as a dog would die, by the wayside as we go.

One by one they're falling round us, their pale faces
    to the sky;
We've no strength left to dig them graves—there let
    them lie.
The wild bird, if he's stricken, is mourned by the
    others,
But we—we die in Christian land,—we die amid our
    brothers,
In a land which God has given us, like a wild beast in
    his cave,
Without a tear, a prayer, a shroud, a coffin, or a grave.
Ha! but think ye the contortions on each livid face
    ye see,
Will not be read on Judgement-day by eyes of Deity?

We are wretches, famished, scorned, human tools to
    build your pride,
But God will yet take vengeance for the souls for
    whom Christ died.
Now in your hour of pleasure—bask ye in the world's
    caress;
But our whitening bones against ye will rise as witnesses,
From the cabins and the ditches in their charred,
    uncoffined masses,

For the Angel of the Trumpet will know them as he
    passes.
A ghastly spectral army, before the great God we'll stand,
And arraign ye as our murderers, the spoilers of our
    land!

My Grave

Thomas Osborne Davis

Shall they bury me in the deep,
Where wind-forgetting waters sleep?
Shall they dig a grave for me
Under the green-wood tree?
Or on the wild heath,
Where the wilder breath
Of the storm doth blow?
Oh, no! oh, no!

Shall they bury me in the palace tombs,
Or under the shade of cathedral domes?
Sweet 'twere to lie on Italy's shore;
Yet not there—nor in Greece, though I love it more.
In the wolf or the vulture my grave shall I find?
Shall my ashes career on the world-seeing wind?
Shall they fling my corpse in the battle mound,
Where coffinless thousands lie under the ground—

Just as they fall they are buried so?
Oh, no! oh, no!

No! on an Irish green-hill side,
On an opening lawn, but not too wide!
For I love the drip of the wetted trees;
I love not the gales, but a gentle breeze
To freshen the turf; put no tombstone there,
But green sods, decked with daisies fair;
Nor sods too deep, but so that the dew
The matted grass-roots may trickle through.
Be my epitaph writ on my country's mind:
"He served his country, and loved his kind."
Oh! 'twere merry unto the grave to go,
If one were sure to be buried so.

The Irish Mother's Lament

Cecil Frances Alexander

Half the long night, my children, I lie waking
    Till the dawn rustles in the old thorn-tree,
Then dream of you, while the red morn is breaking
    Beyond that broad salt sea;

In this poor room, where many a time the measure
    Of your low, regular breathing in mine ear,

Brought to my listening heart a keener pleasure
    Than any music clear;

Here, where, your soft heads in my bosom laying,
    Ye nestled, with your hearts to my heart press'd;
And I have felt your little fingers playing,
    All night, around my breast;

On the brown hill-side, where so oft together,
    Roaming forth idly, when our work was done,
We heard the moor-fowl in the purple heather,
    Crowing at set of sun;

I am alone—still on my threshold lieth
    The shadow of the thorn ye play'd beneath,
Still to her mate, at eve, the brown bird crieth,
    Out of the lonely heath:

But in my desolate house no sound of laughter,
    And by my dreary hearth no daughter's face;
I watch the black smoke curling round the rafter,
    I see each empty place.

How could ye leave me? Did ye think a mother
    Was natured like a bird in summer's prime,
Who leaves her young brood, hopeful of another
    In the next glad spring time?

They tell me your new home is rich and sunny,
    More than this dwelling on the mountain cold,

Fair as the land that flowed with milk and honey,
In the great Book of old.

They tell me flowers most beautiful are blowing
Out on your waysides, on your common trees,
But will ye find the mother's love there growing,
Ye gave for things like these?

And some have told me souls are never parted,
Faith leads us all unto the same bright Heaven,
Nor meet it is, that woman, Christian-hearted,
To such wild grief be given;

Ah! But I know in that bright land is wanting
On Sunday morn, the sweet church-calling bell,
The pastoral word, the gather'd voices chanting
Hymns that ye loved so well.

The cares of this great world, its toils, its beauty,
Will dim your eyes, and grow about your heart,
And shut out heavenly hope and Christian duty,
And every better part.

The prayers we pray'd together at God's altar,
The creed ye lisp'd into my ear at night,
The verses that I taught your lips to falter
Will be forgotten quite.

Ah me! could I but think those lips were making,
In some far church, the vows they used to pour,

I could lie down without this wild heart-aching
   Lest we should meet no more.

Sad mother! for the visible presence pining
  Of eyes that smile, and lips that fondly move,
Things that, like dewy nights and bright sun's
  shining,
    Nurse the sweet flowers of love.

But, sadder far, when the wild waves that sever,
  Sing to her ear in one foreboding strain:—
"We part you now, but must ye part for ever?"
   Echoing the heart's dull pain.

To God and Ireland True

Ellen O'Leary

I sit beside my darling's grave,
  Who in the prison died,
And tho' my tears fall thick and fast,
  I think of him with pride:—
Ay, softly fall my tears like dew,
For one to God and Ireland true.

"I love my God o'er all," he said,
  "And then I love my land,

And next I love my Lily sweet,
    Who pledged me her white hand:—
To each—to all—I'm ever true,
To God—to Ireland and to you."

No tender nurse his hard bed smoothed
    Or softly raised his head:—
He fell asleep and woke in heaven
    Ere I knew he was dead;—
Yet why should I my darling rue?
He was to God and Ireland true.

O, 'tis a glorious memory;
    I'm prouder than a queen
To sit beside my hero's grave
    And think on what has been:—
And O, my darling, I am true
To God—to Ireland and to you!

The Memory of the Dead

John Kells Ingram

Who fears to speak of Ninety-eight?
    Who blushes at the name?
When cowards mock the patriot's fate,
    Who hangs his head for shame?

He's all a knave or half a slave
    Who slights his country thus;
But a true man, like you, man,
    Will fill your glass with us.

We drink the memory of the brave,
    The faithful and the few—
Some lie far off beyond the wave,
    Some sleep in Ireland, too;
All, all are gone—but still lives on
    The fame of those who died;
All true men, like you, men,
    Remember them with pride.

Some on the shores of distant lands
    Their weary hearts have laid,
And by the stranger's heedless hands
    Their lonely graves were made;
But, though their clay be far away
    Beyond the Atlantic foam,
In true men, like you, men,
    Their spirit's still at home.

The dust of some is Irish earth;
    Among their own they rest;
And the same land that gave them birth
    Has caught them to her breast;
And we will pray that from their clay
    Full many a race may start

Of true men, like you, men,
    To act as brave a part.

They rose in dark and evil days
    To right their native land;
They kindled here a living blaze
    That nothing shall withstand.
Alas! that Might can vanquish Right—
    They fell, and passed away;
But true men, like you, men,
    Are plenty here to-day.

Then here's their memory—may it be
    For us a guiding light,
To cheer our strife for liberty,
    And teach us to unite!
Through good and ill, be Ireland's still,
    Though sad as theirs your fate;
And true men, be you, men,
    Like those of Ninety-Eight.

Dark Rosaleen

James Clarence Mangan (Translator)

O my dark Rosaleen,
    Do not sigh, do not weep!

The priests are on the ocean green,
    They march along the deep.
There's wine from the royal Pope,
    Upon the ocean green;
And Spanish ale shall give you hope,
    My dark Rosaleen!
    My own Rosaleen!
Shall glad your heart, shall give you hope,
Shall give you health and help, and hope,
    My Dark Rosaleen.

Over hills, and through dales,
    Have I roamed for your sake;
All yesterday I sailed with sails
    On river and on lake.
The Erne, at its highest flood,
    I dashed across unseen,
For there was lightning in my blood,
    My dark Rosaleen!
    My own Rosaleen!
Oh! there was lightning in my blood,
Red lightning lightened through my blood,
    My Dark Rosaleen!

All day long in unrest,
    To and fro do I move,
The very soul within my breast
    Is wasted for you, love!
The heart in my bosom faints
    To think of you, my Queen,

My life of life, my saint of saints.
    My dark Rosaleen!
    My own Rosaleen!
To hear your sweet and sad complaints,
My life, my love, my saint of saints,
    My Dark Rosaleen!

Woe and pain, pain and woe,
    Are my lot, night and noon,
To see your bright face clouded so,
    Like to the mournful moon.
But yet will I rear your throne
    Again in golden sheen;
'Tis you shall reign, shall reign alone,
    My dark Rosaleen!
    My own Rosaleen!
'Tis you shall have the golden throne,
'Tis you shall reign, shall reign alone,
    My Dark Rosaleen!

Over dews, over sands,
    Will I fly for your weal:
Your holy, delicate white hands
    Shall girdle me with steel.
At home in your emerald bowers,
    From morning's dawn till e'en,
You'll pray for me, my flower of flowers,
    My dark Rosaleen!
    My fond Rosaleen!

You'll think of me through daylight's hours,
My virgin flower, my flower of flowers,
 My Dark Rosaleen!

I could scale the blue air,
 I could plough the high hills,
Oh, I could kneel all night in prayer,
 To heal your many ills!
And one beamy smile from you
 Would float like light between
My toils and me, my own, my true,
 My dark Rosaleen!
 My fond Rosaleen!
Would give me life and soul anew,
A second life, a soul anew,
 My Dark Rosaleen!

O! the Erne shall run red
 With redundance of blood,
The earth shall rock beneath our tread,
 And flames wrap hill and wood,
And gun-peal, and slogan cry
 Wake many a glen serene,
Ere you shall fade, ere you shall die,
 My dark Rosaleen!
 My own Rosaleen!
The Judgment Hour must first be nigh
Ere you can fade, ere you can die,
 My Dark Rosaleen!

Lament for the Poets: 1916

Francis Ledwidge

I heard the Poor Old Woman say:
"At break of day the fowler came,
And took my blackbirds from their songs
Who loved me well thro' shame and blame.

"No more from lovely distances
Their songs shall bless me mile by mile,
Nor to white Ashbourne call me down
To wear my crown another while.

"With bended flowers the angels mark
For the skylark the place they lie,
From there its little family
Shall dip their wings first in the sky.

"And when the first surprise of flight
Sweet songs excite, from the far dawn
Shall there come blackbirds loud with love,
Sweet echoes of the singers gone.

"But in the lonely hush of eve
Weeping I grieve the silent bills."
I heard the Poor Old Woman say
In Derry of the little hills.

An Irish Beauty

Ellen Forrester

Dark eyes softly beaming, and pearly teeth gleaming,
    And black rippling tresses, loose, flowing, and free;
A face sweet and simple, and many an arch dimple—
    That's Nora, my Nora, sweet Nora Magee.

A small foot, a neat foot, a dainty and fleet foot,
    No foot in the dance half so nimble you'd see;
As gay as a fairy, and graceful and airy—
    That's Nora, my Nora, sweet Nora Magee.

Now teasing, now vexing, and always perplexing
    The heart that adores her to such a degree;
Now frowning, now smiling, bewitching, beguiling—
    That's Nora, my Nora, sweet Nora Magee.

Dark eyes softly beaming, and pearly teeth gleaming,
    Capricious, and wilful, and charming is she;
In kind mood or cruel, she's always my jewel—
    My own darling Nora, sweet Nora Magee.

Kathleen O'More

George Nugent Reynolds

My love, still I think that I see her once more,
But, alas! she has left me her loss to deplore—
   My own little Kathleen, my poor little Kathleen,
      My Kathleen O'More!

Her hair glossy black, her eyes were dark blue,
Her colour still changing, her smiles ever new—
   So pretty was Kathleen, my sweet little Kathleen,
      My Kathleen O'More!

She milked the dun cow, that ne'er offered to stir;
Though wicked to all, it was gentle to her—
   So kind was my Kathleen, my poor little Kathleen,
      My Kathleen O'More!

She sat at the door one cold afternoon,
To hear the wind blow, and to gaze on the moon,—
   So pensive was Kathleen, my poor little Kathleen,
      My Kathleen O'More!

Cold was the night-breeze that sighed round her bower,
It chilled my poor Kathleen, she drooped from that
     hour,
   And I lost my poor Kathleen, my own little
   Kathleen,
      My Kathleen O'More!

The bird of all birds that I love the best
Is the robin that in the churchyard builds his nest;
   For he seems to watch Kathleen, hops lightly o'er
     Kathleen,
        My Kathleen O'More.

Rory O'More

Samuel Lover

Young Rory O'More courted Kathleen bán,
He was bold as a hawk,—and she soft as the dawn;
He wished in his heart pretty Kathleen to please,
And he thought the best way to do that was to tease;
"Now Rory, be aisy," sweet Kathleen would cry—
Reproof on her lip, but a smile in her eye;
"With your tricks, I don't know, in troth, what I'm
   about;
Faith, you've teased me till I've put on my cloak
   inside out";
"Och, jewel," says Rory, "that same is the way
You've thrated my heart for this many a day,
And 'tis plased that I am, and why not, to be sure?
For 'tis all for good luck," says bold Rory O'More.

"Indeed, then," says Kathleen, "don't think of the like,
For I half gave a promise to soothering Mike;

The ground that I walk on, he loves, I'll be bound."
"Faith," says Rory, "I'd rather love you than the
    ground."
"Now, Rory, I'll cry, if you don't let me go;
Sure I dhrame every night that I'm hating you so."
"Och," says Rory, "that same I'm delighted to hear,
For dhrames always go by contraries, my dear;
So, jewel, keep dhramin' that same till you die,
And bright mornin' will give dirty night the black lie;
And 'tis plased that I am, and why not, to be sure?
Since 'tis all for good luck," says bold Rory O'More.

"Arrah, Kathleen, my darlint, you've teased me
    enough,
And I've thrashed for your sake Dinny Grimes and
    James Duff,
And I've made myself, drinkin' your health, quite a
    baste,
So I think, after that, I may talk to the priest."
Then Rory, the rogue, stole his arm round her neck,
So soft and so white, without freckle or speck,
And he looked in her eyes that were beaming with
    light.
And he kissed her sweet lips—don't you think he
    was right?
"Now, Rory, leave off, sir; you'll hug me no more;
That's eight times to-day that you've kissed me before."
"Then here goes another," says he, "to make sure,
For there's luck in odd numbers," says Rory O'More.

Donal Kenny

John Keegan Casey

"Come, piper, play the 'Shaskan Reel,'
    Or else the 'Lasses on the Heather,'
And, Mary, lay aside your wheel
    Until we dance once more together.
At fair and pattern oft before
    Of reels and jigs we've tripped full many;
But ne'er again this loved old floor
    Will feel the foot of Donal Kenny."

Softly she rose and took his hand,
    And softly glided through the measure,
While, clustering round the village band
    Looked half in sorrow, half in pleasure.
Warm blessings flowed from every lip
    As ceased the dancers' airy motion:
O Blessed Virgin! guide the ship
    Which bears bold Donal o'er the ocean!

"Now God be with you all!" he sighed,
    Adown his face the bright tears flowing—
"God guard you well, avick," they cried,
    "Upon the strange path you are going."
So full his breast, he scarce could speak,
    With burning grasp the stretched hands taking,
He pressed a kiss on every cheek,
    And sobbed as if his heart was breaking.

"Boys, don't forget me when I'm gone,
    For sake of all the days passed over—
The days you spent on heath and bawn,
    With Donal Ruadh, the rattlin' rover.
Mary, agra, your soft brown eye
    Has willed my fate," he whispered lowly;
"Another holds thy heart: good-bye!
    Heaven grant you both its blessings holy!"

A kiss upon her brow of snow,
    A rush across the moonlit meadow,
Whose broom-clad hazels, trembling slow,
    The mossy boreen wrapped in shadow;
Away o'er Tully's bounding rill,
    And far beyond the Inny river;
One cheer on Carrick's rocky hill,
    And Donal Kenny's gone for ever.

The breezes whistled through the sails,
    O'er Galway Bay the ship was heaving,
And smothered groans and bursting wails
    Told all the grief and pain of leaving.
One form among that exiled band
    Of parting sorrow gave no token,
Still was his breath, and cold his hand:
    For Donal Kenny's heart was broken.

The Western Winds
John Walsh

A maiden sat on an ocean-steep;
    She gazed on the place where the sun went down,
Her face was mild as an infant's sleep,
    Her silken hair was a wavy brown.
She murmured sadly, softly, and low,
    As the soothing tone of the gentle dove,
"Of all the winds the heavens can blow,
    The West, the West is the one I love.

"Last night I dreamed that a summer eve
    Brought back my long-lost love to me;
He clasped me close, and 'No longer grieve,'
    He whispered me softly, 'astór machree.'
Alas, alas!" and her voice was low
    As the plaintive tone of the gentle dove,
"The sun is gone, and the West winds blow,
    Yet where, oh! where is my plighted love?

"'Tis a long dark dream, like a funeral hymn;
    Will it ever end—will it pass away?
My heart is sad, and my eyes are dim;
    Will it ever behold hope's dawning day?"
Her voice sank down to an accent low
    As the soothing tone of the gentle dove—
"How sweet the rush of the West winds blow!
    But where, ah! where is my only love?

"If Eoghan comes, will he bring to me
    The heart that away from Erin he bore?
They say that all in that land are free,
    And perhaps he may love its maidens more.
Oh no, oh no!" she murmured low,
    As soft as the tone of the plaintive dove;
"The Western wind is the one, I know,
    That will bear me homeward the heart I love.

"Sad was the hour that saw him sail—
    'Twas for life, dear life, he was forced to flee;
Dark was the ship when she bent to the gale,
    For she bore my world, my all from me.
Astór!" she murmured, sad and low
    As the soothing tone of the gentle dove,
"Why did not I to that black ship go,
    And be near you for ever, my absent love?"

Weep not, sweet maid; for his face you will see;
    He will clasp that hand to his own once more;
He will tread o'er his native hills as free
    As he does even now on the distant shore;
For their ranks are full, and their hearts are true,
    And their arms are young, and bold, and brave;
We will see their ships when the sun sinks through
    The golden brim of the Western wave.

O, It Was Out by Donnycarney

James Joyce

O, it was out by Donnycarney
　　When the bat flew from tree to tree
My love and I did walk together;
　　And sweet were the words she said to me.

Along with us the summer wind
　　Went murmuring—O, happily!—
But softer than the breath of summer
　　Was the kiss she gave to me.

Index of First Lines